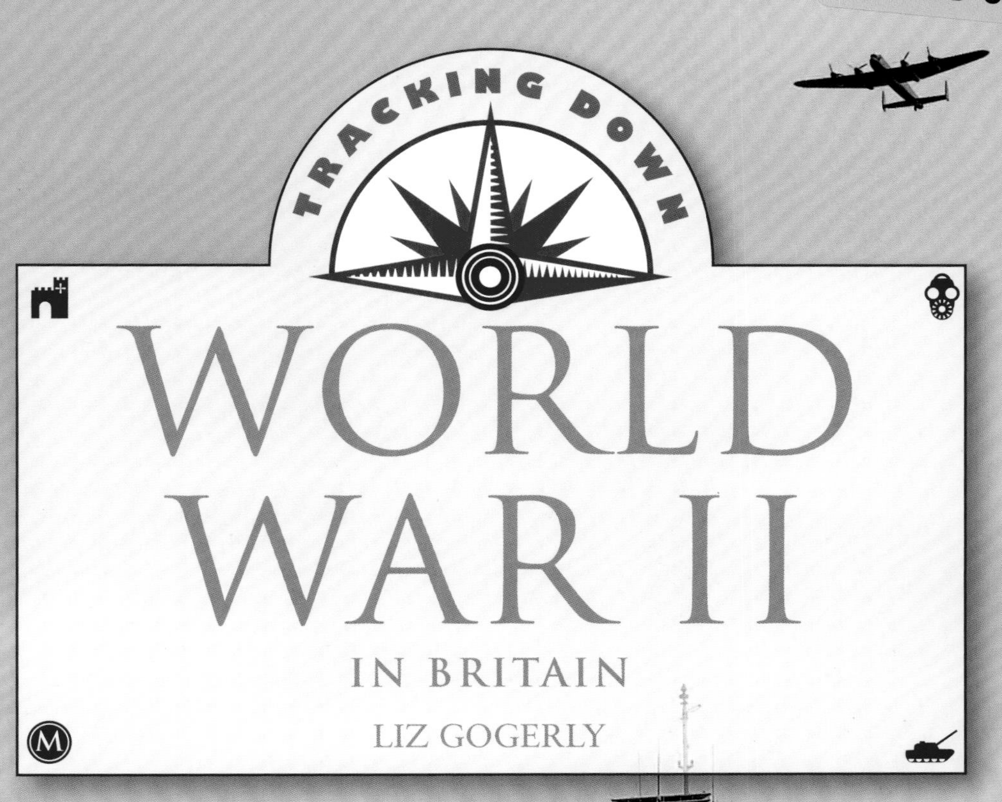

WORLD WAR II

IN BRITAIN

LIZ GOGERLY

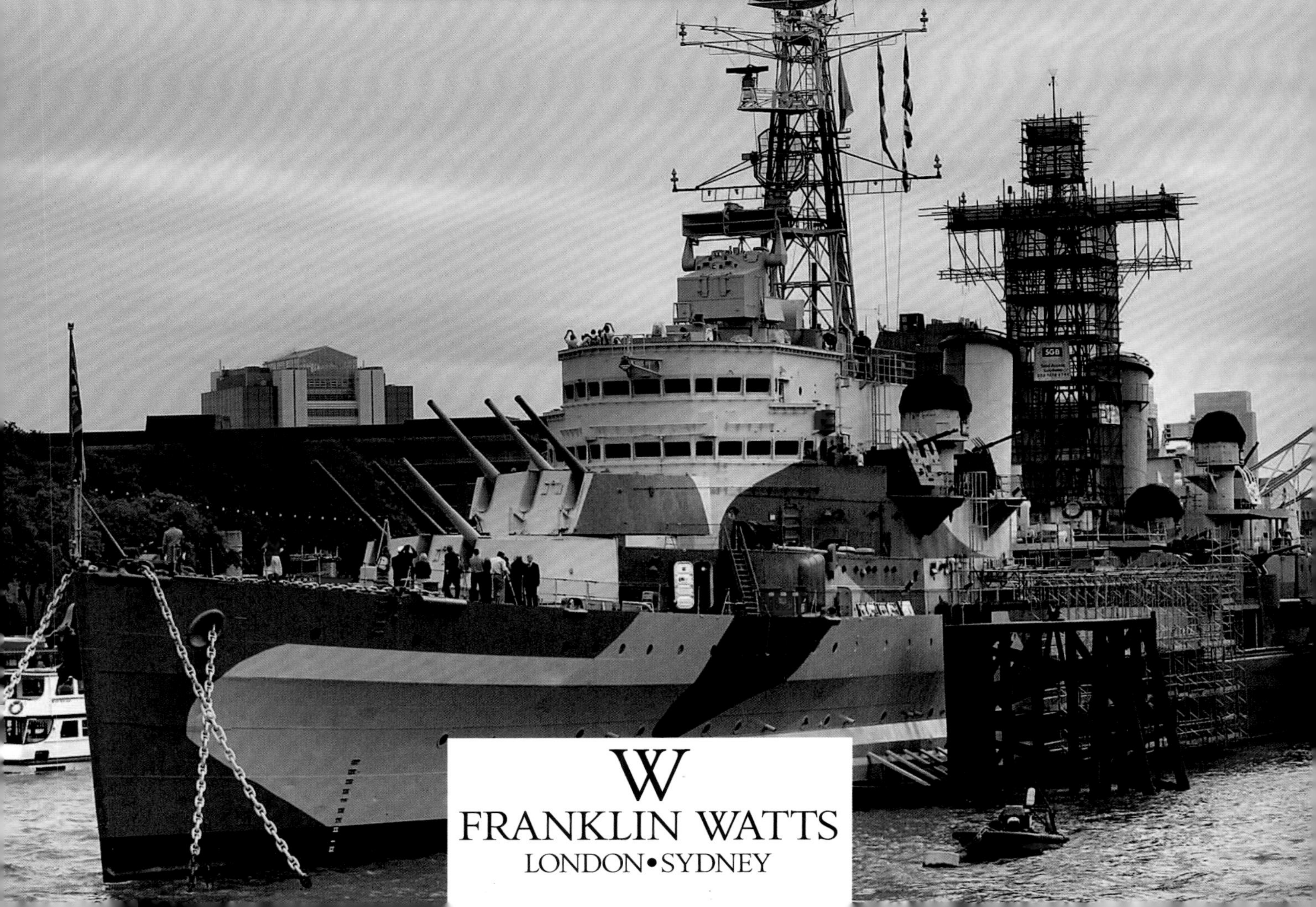

FRANKLIN WATTS
LONDON•SYDNEY

This edition published in 2013 by Franklin Watt

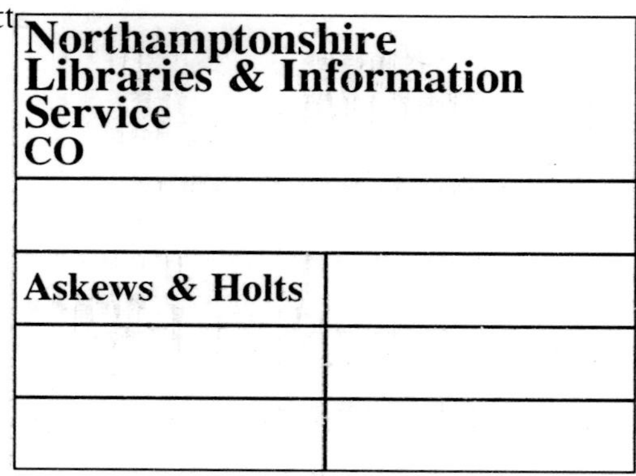
Northamptonshire
Libraries & Information
Service
CO

Askews & Holts

Copyright © 2013 Franklin Watts

Franklin Watts
338 Euston Road
London NW1 3BH

Franklin Watts Australia
Level 17/207 Kent Street
Sydney, NSW 2000

All rights reserved.

A CIP catalogue record for this book is available
from the British Library.

Dewey number: 940.5

ISBN 978 1 4451 1656 3

Printed in China

Franklin Watts is a division of Hachette Children's Books,
an Hachette UK company.

www.hachette.co.uk

Editor: Sarah Ridley
Design: John Christopher/White Design
Editor in Chief: John C. Miles
Art director: Jonathan Hair
Picture research: Diana Morris

Picture credits:
Lt Col Coughlin/Imperial War Museum London: 8t. CS Imagebase/Alamy: 25b. Kayte Deioma: 7t.
Elmtree Images/Alamy: 27b. Paul Harris/Alamy: 8b. Hulton Archive/Getty Images: 5bl, 6. Hulton-Deutsch/Corbis: 15tr, 17b.
Imperial War Museum London: 9, 11tr, 12, 18, 20. Kent Battle of Britain Museum Hawkinge Kent: 11bl. Keystone/Hulton Archive/Getty Images: 22. Barry Lewis/Corbis: 13. Paul Libera/Corbis: 10. Peter Macdiamid/Getty Images: front cover, 1.
Steve Nichols/Alamy: 26t. Pictorial Press /Alamy: 21tr. Picturepoint/Topham: 14, 19t. Popperfoto/Getty Images: 7b.
RIA Novosti/Topfoto: 24tr. Rolf Richardson/Alamy: 21bl. Royal Navy Submarine Museum, Gosport: 23b.
Robert Sargent/Lightroom Photos/USCG/Topfoto: 25t. Brian Stark/Alamy: 27t. Lee Karen Stow/Alamy: 17t.
Israel Talby/PD: 15bl. The Tank Museum Bovington Dorset: 24bl. Topfoto: 5tr, 19b, 26bl. UK City Images/Topfoto: 23t.
Ullsteinbild/Topfoto: 4. Maciej Wojtkowiak/Alamy: 16.

Every attempt has been made to clear copyright. Should there be any inadvertent omission please apply to the publisher for rectification.

CONTENTS

WHAT WAS WORLD WAR II? 6
RUNNING THE WAR 8
DEFENDING BRITAIN 10
THE BATTLES IN THE SKY 12
EARLY WARNING SYSTEMS 14
AIR-RAID SHELTERS 16
LIFE ON THE HOME FRONT 18
THE CHILDREN'S WAR 20
WOMEN IN ACTION 22
THE WAR AT SEA 24
THE NORMANDY LANDINGS 26
THE END OF THE WAR 28
GLOSSARY 30
PLACES TO VISIT 31
INDEX 32

WHAT WAS WORLD WAR II?

World War II lasted from 1939 to 1945. It was the most widespread world conflict of all time. Life changed for everybody living in Britain. You can find out what life was like by tracking down the evidence around you.

Why the war began

In 1933 Adolf Hitler became Chancellor of Germany. He was ambitious and wanted to make Germany the biggest empire in the world. In March 1939 he ordered the German army to invade Czechoslovakia, followed by Poland on 1 September 1939. Britain and France demanded that Hitler withdraw his troops. Hitler ignored their demands. Suddenly, the threat of a German invasion of Britain and other European countries became a real possibility.

◆ Nazi troops and tanks invade Poland in September 1939.

War is declared

At 11.15 am on 3 September 1939 the British prime minister, Neville Chamberlain, made an announcement on the radio. In a solemn voice he said, "... this country is at war with Germany." Less than ten minutes later the air-raid sirens in London were wailing. It was only a test run but the sound sent a chill through Londoners. Hitler's bombers could target them at any moment.

The headline speaks for itself in this view of a London newspaper seller on 3 September 1939.

GO VISIT

The Imperial War Museum, London

You can visit your local museum to find about World War II in your area. However, the Imperial War Museum (IWM) in London has the largest collection of photographs, paintings and artefacts from the war. You can see aeroplanes, artillery and firearms.

Londoners wearing their gas masks, from a photo in the Imperial War Museum.

Preparing for the worst

Britain was not unprepared for war but there was work to be done. In the previous months millions of people had been issued with gas masks, in case the Germans dropped gas bombs. An elaborate plan, called Operation Pied Piper, had been made to evacuate millions of children from towns and cities to safer places in the countryside. Between 1 and 4 September this plan swung into action. In addition, buses, railways and army vehicles were crammed with soldiers on the move. Everybody was talking about the war. People were frightened but they were determined to stop Hitler.

RUNNING THE WAR

Everybody had a part to play in defending Britain but there needed to be a strong leader. In May 1940 politician and ex-army officer, Winston Churchill, became Prime Minister.

The 'Phoney War'

In September 1939 people prepared themselves for the worst. They expected Hitler to bomb Britain and they waited to hear news of major fighting in Europe. For nearly eight months nothing seemed to happen. This became known as the 'Phoney War'. Then in April 1940 Germany invaded Denmark and Norway. On 10 May Winston Churchill became Prime Minister. The same day Germany invaded France, Belgium, the Netherlands and Luxembourg. In the next few months Churchill made speeches which inspired Britons to stand up and fight.

▼ British Prime Minister Winston Churchill, pictured during the war.

"... I have nothing to offer but blood, toil, tears and sweat. We have before us an ordeal of the most grievous kind. We have before us many, many long months of struggle and suffering..."

Winston Churchill, speaking to the House of Commons, 13 May 1940

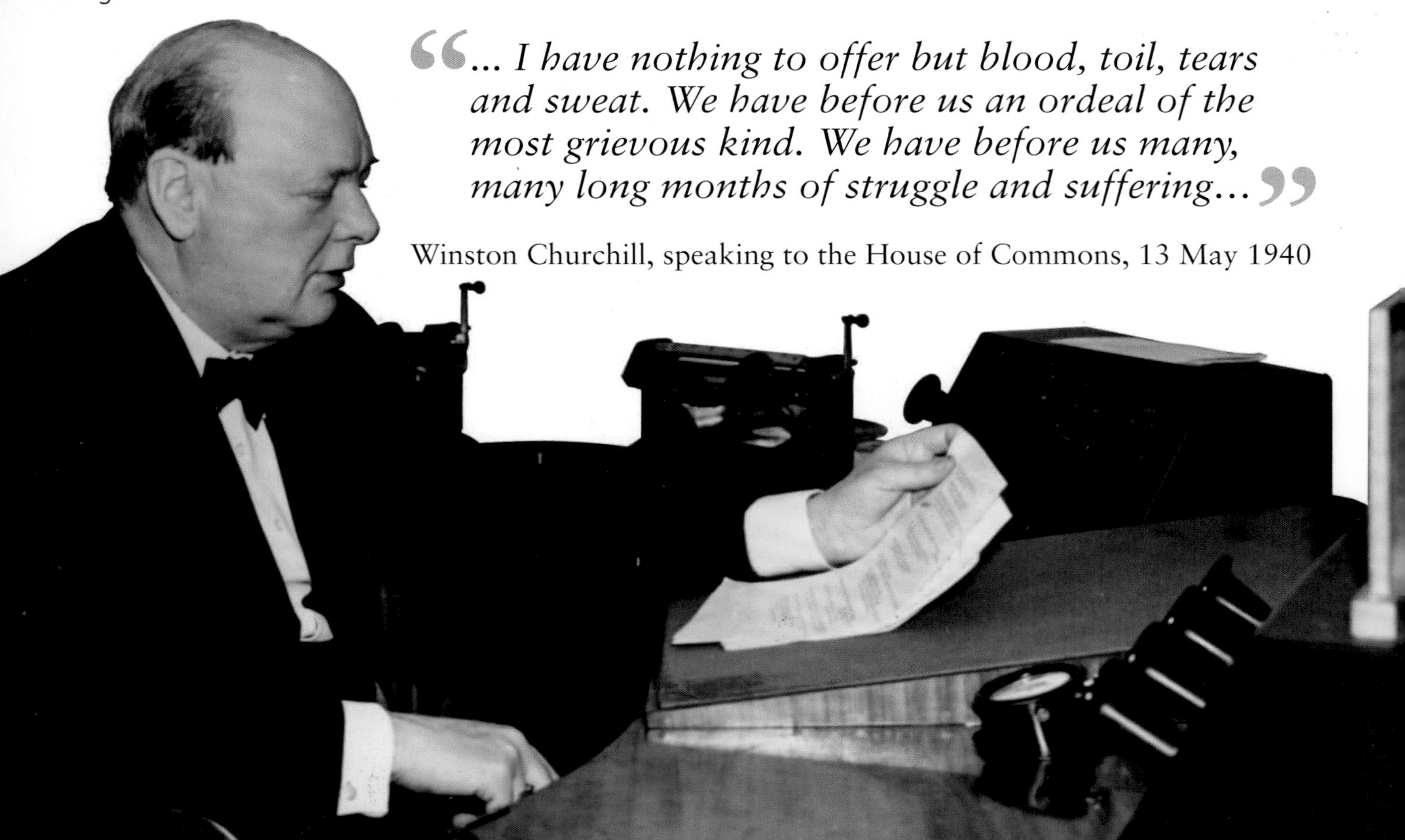

↑ Staff in the Map Room at the Cabinet War Rooms kept track of all aspects of the war.

The Cabinet War Rooms

Churchill made many of his wartime speeches from an underground bunker in Whitehall, London. The bunker was built in 1939 as an air-raid shelter for the Prime Minister and members of the War Cabinet. It was from here that the cabinet could continue the important business of running the war when London was under attack. He made some of his speeches from the office-bedroom, which is equipped with radio microphones. Today, the Cabinet War Rooms are a museum and look much the same as they did during the war.

GO VISIT

Western Approaches, Liverpool War Museum

In 1941 a bomb-proof bunker in Liverpool became home for the Western Approaches. It was their job to monitor enemy ships and U-boats at sea in order to protect the ships bringing vital food, supplies and troops to Britain. These secret underground rooms were staffed by the Royal Navy, Royal Air Force and Royal Marines and are now a museum.

Senior officers confer at Western Approaches during the war.

DEFENDING BRITAIN

At the end of May 1940, British and Allied troops trapped by the advance of the Germans were evacuated from Dunkirk. The threat of a German invasion seemed more real. The same month, a massive building project to defend Britain began.

→ A soldier defends a camouflaged pillbox in this wartime view.

Pillboxes

These mini-forts were small concrete buildings, nicknamed 'pillboxes' because of their shape. In the early years of the war, soldiers and other volunteers built about 28,000 pillboxes along coastlines, near airfields, canals and roads. They were camouflaged to blend in with the local landscape using paint, pebbles, leaves and branches. Most pillboxes were used by reserve soldiers or members of the Home Guard who would have defended Britain against invading Germans. There are about 6,000 pillboxes left in Britain so you may be lucky enough to find one that is still in good condition near you.

↓ Pillboxes were placed in key locations, often near the coast, as here on Mersea Island in Essex.

▲ A coastal gun emplacement at Dover, Kent, fires its guns in December 1942. These guns were designed to halt German invaders.

Vehicle obstacles

Britain also prepared itself against a German invasion by building vehicle obstacles to stop tanks and other army vehicles. Many of these defences were just rows of concrete blocks. They were placed along beaches, on bridges or near railways. Many were removed after the war but it's still possible to find them, especially on coastlines. At Fairbourne Beach, Merioneth, Gwynedd, North Wales, there is a line of concrete blocks that were built to protect the coastline. In south Liverpool a row of anti-tank blocks, nicknamed Dragons Teeth (or Pimples) because they were pointed, are hidden amongst the undergrowth by the railway line.

GO VISIT

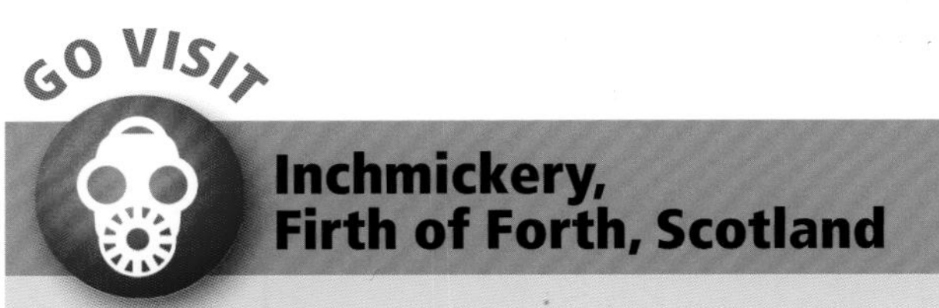

Inchmickery, Firth of Forth, Scotland

Just north of Edinburgh in the Firth of Forth lies the tiny island of Inchmickery. Nobody lives there today but pillboxes, military buildings and a jetty built during the war are still standing. From a distance the buildings look like a World War II battleship. You can take a boat trip around the island, which is now a bird reserve.

By the summer of 1940 Hitler believed that Germany would soon defeat Britain. His plan was to destroy the Royal Air Force (RAF) then invade Britain.

The Battle of Britain

The Battle of Britain was a series of air battles fought over Britain. It lasted from 10 July until 31 October 1940. The *Luftwaffe*, the German air force, concentrated its first wave of attacks on ships in the English Channel. Later it raided airfields on the coast and radar stations before moving to inland airfields, aircraft factories and major ports. The Luftwaffe was stronger than the RAF, but the RAF triumphed and Hitler turned his attention away from Britain.

▼ The Battle of Britain Monument on the Embankment in London commemorates the men and women of the RAF who defended Britain.

↓ The Spitfire was key to winning the Battle of Britain.

GO VISIT

Spitfires and Hurricanes

Two British fighter aircraft that played a major role in the Battle of Britain were the Hawker Hurricane and the Supermarine Spitfire. You can see Hurricanes and Spitfires at RAF Coningsby in Lincolnshire. This World War II airfield is still in use and is home to the Battle of Britain Memorial Flight. You can also see many historic aircraft on display and flying at Duxford.

Airports

RAF squadrons were stationed at airfields throughout Britain. Airfields in the south were the most heavily attacked by the Germans. These included RAF Biggin Hill and RAF Debden which are still in use today. RAF Duxford is now home to the Imperial War Museum Duxford. Inside one of the hangars there is an exhibition about the Battle of Britain.

↑ Aircraft on display at the Kent Battle of Britain Museum, near Folkestone. The museum is a former RAF airfield.

Temporary airfields

Hundreds of temporary airstrips were built during the war on farmland that was taken over by the government. These airfields were abandoned after the war but evidence of their existence may still be there, such as old hangars, control towers, fuel stores and landing strips. Find out whether there were RAF airfields near you and if anything remains.

EARLY WARNING SYSTEMS

The RAF was able to challenge many German air raids using a clever new invention called Radio Detection and Ranging, or radar.

➜ Members of the WAAF at a radar station during the war. Radar was vital to Britain's air defence.

Radar

Developed in the 1930s by British scientists, radar uses radio waves to locate aircraft and ships. During the Battle of Britain and the Blitz, the RAF was supplied with information from a chain of radar stations along the coast. Many women from the Women's Auxiliary Air Force (WAAF) worked at these radar stations. They plotted the movements of German aircraft on maps. This information meant the RAF knew when to scramble their planes. Some historians believe that radar helped Britain to win the Battle of Britain (see page 12).

The first radar stations

The first Chain Home Radar Station was opened at Bawdsey Manor House in Suffolk during 1936. It was here that scientists worked in secret developing the first radar system in the world. Bawdsey was an important link in the chain of radar stations used during the Battle of Britain. It survived the war but its transmitter towers fell down in 2000. However, you can still see the transmitter and receiver blocks and the underground bunkers used during the war. To experience what it might have been like to work in a radar station you can visit the RAF Air Defence Radar Museum in Norfolk.

The Listening Ears, Greatstone, Kent

Before radar, Britain experimented with another early warning system. Large concrete 'listening ears' or 'sound mirrors' were built along parts of the coast. Enemy aircraft could be detected from about 43 kilometres away. The system had limited success and when radar was invented in 1935 the 'listening ears' were abandoned. The best examples can be found near Dungeness in Kent.

▼ Modern radar installations, like this one at the RAF Air Defence Radar Museum, are descendants of systems first developed during World War II.

AIR-RAID SHELTERS

In August 1940 the RAF bombed Berlin, the capital of Germany. Hitler hit back with air raids on London and other major cities. British civilians found different ways to shelter from the bombs.

The Blitz

On 7 September 1940 the East End of London was heavily bombarded day and night. The Blitz of Britain had begun. Londoners suffered 57 nights of air raids in a row. Meanwhile, ports, industrial centres and cities such as Coventry, Manchester, Sheffield and Glasgow were also targeted. By May 1941, over 43,000 civilians had been killed. Despite these heavy losses the British refused to surrender to the Germans.

↓ The Blitz caused massive damage to civilian and military targets. Here, rescue workers try to cope with the aftermath of an air raid.

Shelters at home

When the air-raid sirens went off, everyone rushed to an air-raid shelter. Some families had shelters at home. In early 1939 the government began distributing Anderson shelters. These shelters were made from steel panels, placed in a deep hole in the garden. Some shelters survive today as people used them as sheds after the war. Many people did not have gardens so they were provided with Morrison shelters. These box-like shelters were often used as tables.

▲ A family, equipped with gas masks in cardboard boxes, head to their Anderson shelter during an air raid.

GO VISIT

Chistlehurst Caves, Bromley, Kent

One of the most unusual places used as an air-raid shelter is Chistlehurst Caves in Bromley, Kent. This old chalk mine has more than 32 kilometres of tunnels. They provided shelter for over 15,000 people. At the time the caves had electric lighting, a hospital and a chapel but today special tours are given using torches and lamps.

Public shelters

Many schools and factories had shelters built so life could carry on as normal. Stockport Air Raid Shelters in Greater Manchester is a good example of a public shelter and it is now restored to its original condition. Built in 1938, the shelters had room for about 6,500 people. They had electric lighting, a sick bay, toilets and a canteen that was run by the Women's Voluntary Service. Every town had its own public shelters. You could try to discover where they were located in your local area. In London people often took refuge in tube stations.

LIFE ON THE HOME FRONT

Hitler called off the Blitz of Britain in May 1941. The air raids mostly stopped but the British people had other things to worry about at home.

GO VISIT

St Fagans National History Museum, Cardiff, Wales

St Fagans National History Museum in Cardiff is an open-air museum. You can find many buildings from different eras that have been re-erected here. The tiny post office is set up as it would have been during World War II. It has a radio receiver from the War Department for receiving urgent messages.

The home front experience

Food rationing began in January 1940 and later in the war there was clothes rationing. Everybody had to remember to take their gas mask everywhere they went. At night they had to obey the blackout restrictions. Finding out about what it was like to live with these changes is quite different to tracking down places. Talking to people who lived through the war is a good place to start. Diaries and journals can also be discovered in local museums. The Internet is another excellent place to collect evidence.

→ The Post Office at St Fagans Museum retains its authentic wartime atmosphere.

A view inside Eden Camp, showing some of the huts where the POWs lived.

Eden Camp

Another way of tracking down what life was like is to visit a living museum. Eden Camp was built as a Prisoner of War (POW) camp at Malton, North Yorkshire in 1942. Originally it housed Italian prisoners who built the camp huts and worked on local farms. The camp was abandoned in 1948 but in 1986 the camp was turned into a modern history theme museum. Today there are over thirty different huts to visit. Together the huts help to tell the story of the war.

Step back in time...

In hut one, visitors see what a typical family front room looked like at the beginning of the war. In hut two they can see children being evacuated and a housewife struggling with her rations. Hut five shows the bombed front room they saw in hut one. Hut six reminds us that life was not all doom and gloom. The Eden Camp Music Hall presents a puppet show with puppets representing popular entertainers from the war years such as George Formby and Vera Lynn.

Popular wartime entertainer, Vera Lynn, was known as 'the Forces' sweetheart'.

THE CHILDREN'S WAR

The war lasted just under six years. That is a long time in the life of a child. For many youngsters the war and the changes it brought were part of life and they found many ways to enjoy themselves.

Evacuation

At the beginning of the war nearly two million children were evacuated to safe places in the countryside. Pre-school children and babies were often sent with their mothers but many school children were apart from their families. It was a difficult time yet many children enjoyed the experience. Talking to older people is the best way of discovering more about evacuation. You can also find real children's accounts of the war on the Internet (see page 31 for websites).

↓ Evacuee children disembark from a train in 1939.

Living with rationing

Another grim part of daily life was food rationing. Sugar was rationed, as were sweets. Mothers and their children spent long hours in shopping queues to buy food. Some foods, such as bananas, were not rationed but became difficult to find. Many museums have ration books, food packaging, wartime information leaflets and recipe books from the war years on display.

▲ This picture shows rations for two people for a week. The availability of many foods was strictly controlled.

LOOK FOR

Children's Entertainment

On dark nights, with the blackout restriction in force, the best place to be was home. Children enjoyed listening to Children's Hour on the radio and reading. They also played board games with a war theme. A simple game of darts was more fun if you were aiming at a picture of Hitler. Look out for games produced during the war in local museums or toy museums.

➔ A boy plays at being a soldier. Many children's games and toys were war-related.

Fun and games

Another way to track down what it was like during the war is to study old photographs and magazines. You will see children playing in the streets or on bombsites. Lots of boys collected shrapnel and parts of shot-down planes. Children were also expected to do their bit for the war effort. Many children helped to grow vegetables in the 'Dig For Victory' campaign. Children were enthusiastic recyclers too. Children as young as three collected waste paper and rags or salvaged scrap metal for the war effort.

WOMEN IN ACTION

Life was hard for women during the war. Many women juggled housework with war work or doing their bit for the 'war effort'.

War workers

In December 1941 the government passed the National Service Act. This meant that unmarried women aged between twenty and thirty had to do war work. Later in the war older women and married women were also called up. You can find out what these women did by looking at the recruitment posters that are often displayed in museums. With many men away fighting, women were needed in the workplace, especially in the munitions factories.

The armed forces

Posters for the armed services were more glamorous. Recruitment posters for the Auxiliary Territorial Service (ATS), the Women's Royal Naval Service (WRNS) and the Women's Auxiliary Air Force (WAAF) showed women in smart uniforms. Though women in the armed services were not allowed to fight they were trained to build and repair tanks and aircraft. A few even flew planes, although this was usually from the factories to the airstrips.

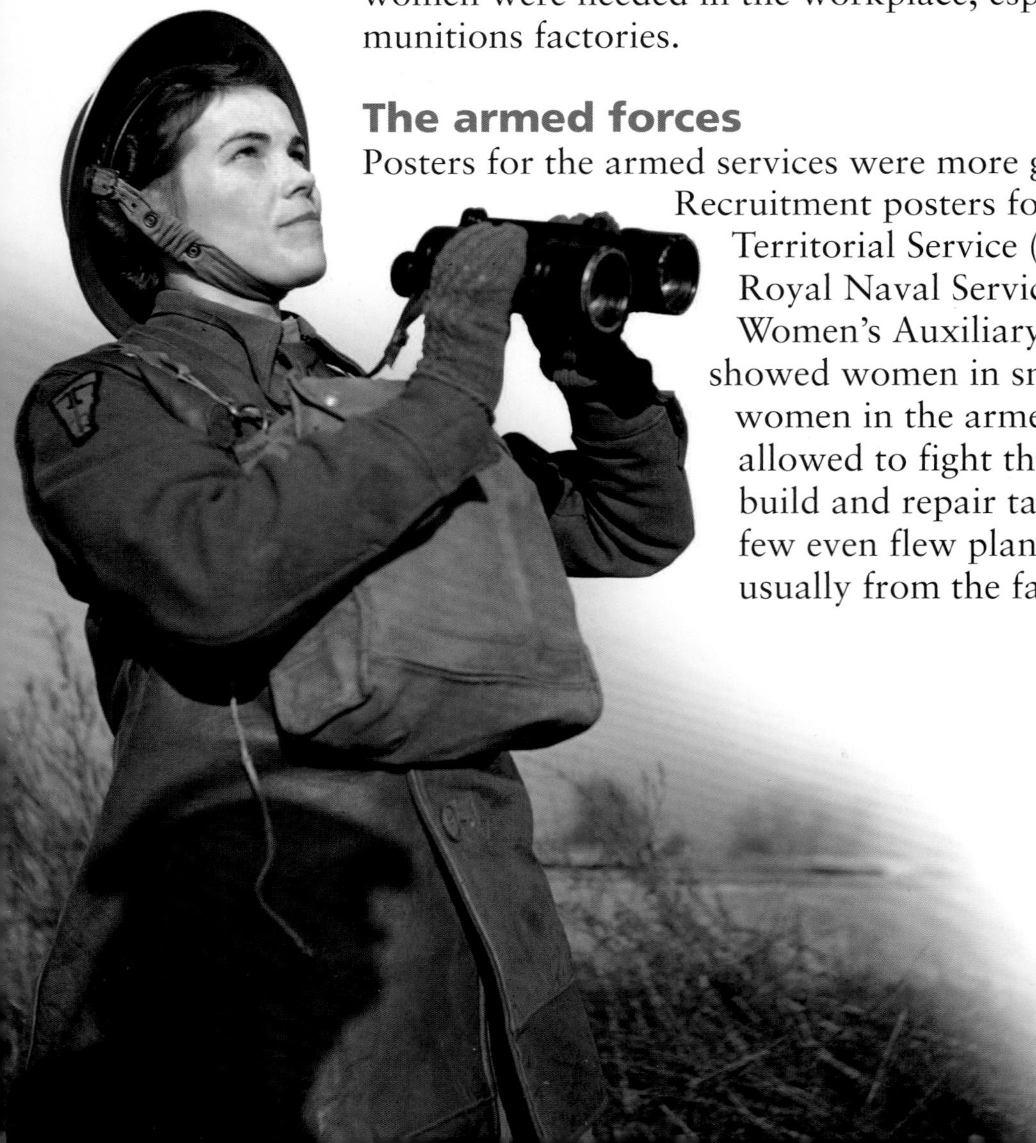

← Women did a wide variety of war work. This member of the ATS is acting as an observer, looking out for enemy aircraft.

Bletchley Park

Some jobs were top secret. Bletchley Park is an old manor house in Buckinghamshire. During the war it was surrounded by high fencing and was the secret centre for British code-breaking. Many of the thousands of code-breakers employed there were women. This wasn't known until recently because the people who worked at Bletchley Park signed the Official Secrets Act. Bletchley Park is now open to the public and you can discover more about some women's important part in helping to break enemy codes during the war.

The 'Colossus' machine, an early computer, helped to crack Nazi codes during the war.

GO VISIT

Memorial to Women at War, Whitehall, London

In 2005 Queen Elizabeth II unveiled the Women at War Memorial in London. The bronze sculpture shows some of the uniforms and working clothes worn by women in World War II. The memorial is the first in Britain to commemorate the millions of women who worked for the war effort. Queen Elizabeth II herself was a member of the ATS during the war.

The striking Women at War Memorial in London's Whitehall.

THE WAR AT SEA

Britain's Royal Navy and Merchant Navy both played a huge part in the war. As an island, Britain was open to attack but the Royal Navy rose to the challenge.

The Battle of the Atlantic

Britain relied upon imported food, raw materials, oil and petrol from America and parts of the British Empire. Hitler planned to cut off these vital supplies by attacking British merchant ships. German submarines (U-boats) fired torpedoes at British ships the day that war was declared. The Royal Navy protected convoys of merchant ships and patrolled the seas hunting for packs of German U-boats. This series of sea battles between the Allies and the Germans was called the Battle of the Atlantic. It was the longest military campaign of the war and lasted until the Germans surrendered in 1945.

↓ A view of a convoy, taken from the deck of a Royal Navy escort vessel.

↑ HMS *Belfast* is part of the Imperial War Museum. She is moored on the River Thames between Tower Bridge and London Bridge in London.

HMS *Belfast*

One British warship that just about survived World War II is HMS *Belfast*. She was mined by German U-boats in 1939 but was back in action two years later. In 1943 she was the most powerful cruiser in the Royal Navy and one of the most important warships in the Atlantic campaign. Today, HMS *Belfast* is a floating museum. Visitors can climb the many sets of steep ladders and stairways to explore all nine decks. They can look inside the kitchen (set up as it was during the war), the navigation rooms and the engine rooms. People are even allowed to climb into one of the gun turrets and aim the anti-aircraft guns.

GO VISIT

Royal Navy Submarine Museum, Gosport, Hampshire

The smallest submarines used by the Royal Navy during the war were called X-Craft. These tiny vessels had to be towed by a full-size submarine to where they were going to be used. You can see inside the only remaining example of these mini submarines at the Royal Navy Submarine Museum at Gosport in Hampshire.

↑ One of the X-Craft mini submarines.

THE NORMANDY LANDINGS

The first day of the Allied invasion of Europe was 6 June 1944. Known as D-Day, Operation Overlord marked the beginning of the end of the war.

The end in sight

In November 1942 the Germans were defeated at Stalingrad by the Russians. By May 1943 the Allies had driven German troops out of North Africa. In September Italy surrendered. In January 1944 the siege of the Russian city of Leningrad finally ended after 890 days of German occupation. Then, in June 1944 the Allies liberated the Italian capital city of Rome from the Germans. The Allies were ready to make an invasion of Nazi-occupied Europe.

→ Victorious Russian soldiers celebrate a Nazi defeat by raising their flag in January 1943.

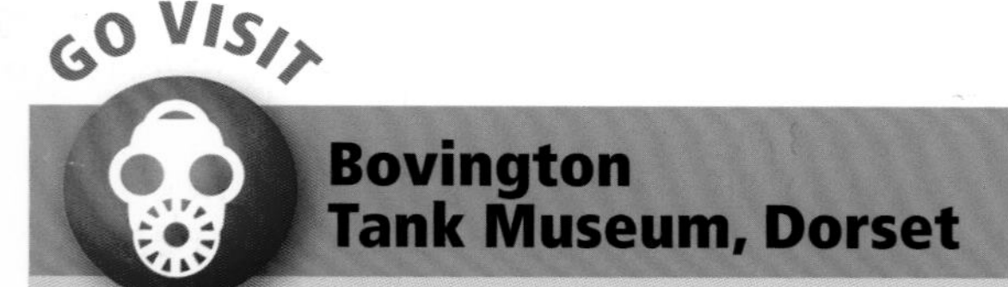

GO VISIT

Bovington Tank Museum, Dorset

During D-Day the Allies used amphibious tanks. Many of these tanks sank during the operation. You can see the only surviving amphibious DD Sherman tank at the Bovington Tank Museum in Dorset.

Operation Overlord

The Allies planned to land their armies in Normandy in France. The operation was given the code name Operation Overlord. On 6 June 1944 over 156,000 troops landed on the beaches at Normandy. By 4 July more than one million Allied troops had arrived in France. Thousands were parachuted in but most came by sea. It was the greatest sea invasion in history. Three months of bitter fighting followed. About 425,000 Allied and German troops are believed to have died. By August the Germans had retreated and the Allies began the liberation of France.

← Soldiers launch an amphibious tank from a landing craft during Operation Overlord.

D-Day Museum

Thousands of Allied ships set sail from Portsmouth, England. Today, you can discover more about the Normandy landings at the D-Day Museum in Portsmouth. The collection includes landing craft, models, maps and photographs of the invasion. The highlight of the exhibition is the Overlord Embroidery. Thirty-four panels measuring 2.4 metres long and 0.9 metres wide tell the story of Operation Overlord. The embroidery was inspired by the ancient Bayeux Tapestry, an embroidery which tells the story of the Norman conquest of England in 1066.

↑ Troops disembark from a landing craft on D-Day to begin retaking occupied Europe.

→ This anti-aircraft gun is on display at the D-Day Museum.

THE END OF THE WAR

An unmanned V1 flying bomb, or 'doodlebug'.

A terrifying Nazi V2 rocket on its launch pad.

Hitler refused to admit defeat and he had one more secret weapon. Once again London and major British cities were in the firing line.

Flying bombs

The V1, nicknamed the 'doodlebug', was a small jet-powered, flying bomb. The Germans fired the first doodlebug at Britain on 13 June 1944, a week after D-Day. Flying bombs were deadly because they were hard to shoot down. Over 6,000 people were killed and 18,000 injured during the V1 strikes.

In September Hitler launched the V2 rocket, a flying bomb that could travel at 5,793 kph. More than a thousand V2 rockets reached Britain, killing over 2,700 people. The attacks came to an end in March 1945 when the Allies destroyed the rocket launching sites. The next month the Allies captured Berlin and defeated Nazi Germany. Hitler committed suicide on 30 April 1945. By 8 May 1945 the war was over in Europe, although fighting continued in the Far East until the Allies dropped terrible atomic bombs on the Japanese cities of Hiroshima and Nagasaki in August. Japan surrendered on 15 August and the war was over.

Houses for the homeless

The V1 and V2 flying bombs destroyed millions of homes. The bombsites and large craters left by the bombs have long been covered over. However, you may still be able to find the prefabricated houses that were built in their place. By 1948, 160,000 prefabricated houses had been erected in Britain. Most of these were made from steel or aluminium. To get an idea of what a 'prefab' was like in the 1940s you can visit the Chilton Open Air Museum. It has a house that is furnished just like it would have been in the 1940s.

➔ Inside the reconstructed 'prefab' at Chilton Open Air Museum.

LOOK FOR

Remembering the war

War memorials help us to remember the dead from World War II. The most famous war memorial in Britain is the Cenotaph in Whitehall, London (right). The Queen and the royal family, together with political and religious leaders, gather here each Remembrance Sunday. Monuments or statues to honour the dead were also erected all over Britain. You could find your local memorial to discover the names of those who died during the war.

Coventry Cathedral was badly bombed in an air raid on 14 November 1940. Although a new cathedral was built, the ruins of the old building were preserved as a memorial to the waste of war, and as a sign of hope for the future.

GLOSSARY

Air raid a bomb attack from the air

Allies Britain, Commonwealth countries, France, Russia and the USA who fought against the Axis powers

Amphibious involving both land and water. Amphibious tanks were designed to move through the sea and on to land

Anderson shelter outdoor air-raid shelter that could be built in the garden

ATS Auxiliary Territorial Service, the women's section of the British army

Axis powers Germany, Italy and Japan and some other Eastern European countries who fought against the Allies

Blackout switching off or concealing all lights, particularly in cities, as a precaution against air raids

Blitz German bombing of British cities. It began in September 1940

Churchill, Winston British prime minister 1940–45

Civilians an ordinary member of the public. Not a soldier or member of other armed forces

Conscription legally calling people to join the services, or do war work

Convoy a group of ships travelling together, with an escort to protect them

Empire lands under the control of a ruling country

Evacuate to move people away from a dangerous place

Evacuee a person who is moved from a dangerous place

First World War (1914–18) also known as World War I

Hitler, Adolf Chancellor of Germany 1933–45

Home Guard a volunteer force of men trained to defend against possible German invasion

Landing craft boats designed to carry soldiers and equipment during attacks from the sea

Luftwaffe the German name for the air force of Nazi Germany

Merchant Navy non-military navy used for commercial and trading purposes, moving goods and equipment around the world

Nazi short for National Socialist. This was an extreme right-wing political party led by Adolf Hitler. It controlled Germany during World War II

Occupied countries countries such as Poland and the Netherlands, which were invaded and occupied by Nazi Germany

Radar stands for Radio Direction and Ranging, originally called RDF (Radio Direction Finding). A system of pinpointing objects using radio waves

RAF Royal Air Force, the British armed air force

Rationing allowing everyone a small fixed amount of something, such as food or petrol, to make certain there is enough for all

Royal Navy British armed naval service

Second World War (1939–45) also known as World War II. Fought between the Axis powers of Germany, Italy and Japan and the Allies, which included Britain, Commonwealth countries, France, Russia and the USA

U-boat stands for *Unterseeboot* (undersea boat), the German word for a military submarine

WAAF women's section of the Royal Air Force

WRNS women's section of the Royal Navy

PLACES TO VISIT

Animals in War Memorial
Brooke Gate, Park Lane,
Hyde Park, London
http://www.indielondon.co.uk/events/att_animals_warmemorial.html

Bawdsey Manor Radar
Bawdsey Manor, Bawdsey, Woodbridge,
Suffolk IP12 3AZ
http://www.bawdseyradar.org.uk

Bletchley Park
The Mansion, Bletchley Park,
Milton Keynes MK3 6EB
http://www.bletchleypark.org.uk

Bovington Tank Museum
Bovington, Dorset BH20 6JG
http://www.tankmuseum.org

Cenotaph
Westminster, London SW1

Chilton Open Air Museum
Newland Park, Gorelands Lane,
Chalfont St Giles,
Buckinghamshire HP8 4AD
http://www.coam.org.uk

Chistlehurst Caves
Old Hill Chislehurst, Kent BR7 5NL
http://www.chislehurstcaves.co.uk

Churchill Museum and Cabinet War Rooms
Clive Steps, King Charles Street,
London SW1A 2AQ
www.iwm.org.uk/visits/churchill-war-rooms

Commando Memorial
Spean Bridge, Nr Fort William, Scotland

D-Day Museum
Portsmouth Museums
and Records Service,
Museum Road,
Portsmouth, Hants PO1 2LJ
http://www.ddaymuseum.co.uk

Eden Camp
Eden Camp Modern History Theme
Museum, Malton, North Yorkshire
YO17 6RT
http://www.edencamp.co.uk

HMS *Belfast*
Morgan's Lane, Tooley Street,
London SE1 2JH
www.iwm.org.uk/visits/hms-belfast

Imperial War Museum
Lambeth Road,
London SE1 6HZ
http://www.iwm.org.uk

Imperial War Museum Duxford
Cambridgeshire CB22 4QR
www.iwm.org.uk/visits/iwm-duxford

Kent Battle of Britain Museum
Aerodrome Road Hawkinge,
Folkestone, Kent CT18 7AG
http://www.kbobm.org

Liverpool War Museum/ The Western Approaches
1-3 Rumford Street (Near Town Hall),
Liverpool L2 3SZ
http://www.liverpoolwarmuseum.co.uk

Memorial to Women at War
Whitehall, London W2

RAF Air Defence Radar Museum
Royal Air Force Neatishead,
Near Horning, Norwich,
Norfolk NR12 8YB
http://www.radarmuseum.co.uk

RAF Coningsby
Lincoln, LN4 4SY
http://www.raf.mod.uk/rafconingsby

Royal Navy Submarine Museum
Haslar Jetty Road,
Gosport, Hampshire PO12 2AS
www.submarine-museum.co.uk/

St Fagans: National History Museum
Cardiff, Wales CF5 6XB
http://www.museumwales.ac.uk/en/stfagans

Stockport Air Raid Shelters
Chestergate, Stockport SK1 1NE
www.stockport.gov.uk/services/leisureculture/visitstockport/museumsandgalleries/airraidshelters/

Thorpe Camp Visitor Centre
Tattershall Thorpe, Lincolnshire
LN4 4PE
http://www.thorpecamp.org.uk

WEBLINKS

Read about a boy's experiences during a V1 raid:
http://www.bbc.co.uk/ww2peopleswar/stories/70/a2732870.shtml

Read real-life accounts of working women during World War II:
http://www.wartimememories.co.uk/women.html

Learn more about children's lives during World War II:
www.bbc.co.uk/schools/primaryhistory/world_war2/children_at_war/

Note to parents and teachers

Every effort has been made by the Publishers to ensure that the websites in this book are suitable for children, that they are of the highest educational value, and that they contain no inappropriate or offensive material. However, because of the nature of the Internet, it is impossible to guarantee that the contents of these sites will not be altered. We strongly advise that Internet access is supervised by a responsible adult.

INDEX

air raids 7, 9, 14, 16-17, 18, 28, 30
airfields 12, 13
Auxiliary Territorial Service (ATS) 22, 23, 30

Battle of the Atlantic 24
Battle of Britain 12-13, 14, 15
Battle of Britain Monument 12
Bawdsey Manor Radar 15
blackout 18, 21, 30
Bletchley Park 23
Blitz 14, 16, 18, 30
bombs, atomic 28
    flying 28, 29
Bovington Tank Museum 26

Cabinet War Rooms 9
camps, POW 19
Cenotaph 29
Chamberlain, N 7
children 7, 19, 20-21
Chilton Open Air Museum 29
Chistlehurst Caves 17
Churchill, W 8, 9, 30
code-breaking 23
convoys 24, 30

D-Day 26-27, 28, 29
D-Day Museum 27
doodlebugs 28
Dunkirk 10

Eden Camp 19
evacuation 7, 10, 19, 20, 30

HMS *Belfast* 25
Hitler, A 6, 7, 8, 12, 16, 18, 21, 24, 28, 30
home front 18-19
houses, prefabricated 29
Hurricanes 13

Imperial War Museum 7, 9, 25
Imperial War Museum Duxford 13
Inchmickery 11
invasion, threat of 6, 10-11, 12

Listening Ears 15
Liverpool War Museum 9
Luftwaffe 12, 30
Lynn, Vera 19

masks, gas 7, 17, 18
Memorial to Women at War 23
memorials, war 29
Merchant Navy 24-25, 30

obstacles, vehicle 11
Operation Overlord 26, 27, 28-29
Operation Pied Piper 7

Phoney War 8
pillboxes 10, 11
prefabs 29

radar 12, 14-15, 30
RAF Air Defence Radar Museum 15
rationing 18, 19, 21, 30
Remembrance Sunday 29
Royal Air Force (RAF) 9, 12, 13, 14, 16, 30
Royal Marines 9
Royal Navy 9, 24-25, 30
Royal Navy Submarine Museum 25

St Fagans National History Museum 18
shelters, air-raid 9, 16-17, 30
siren, air-raid 7, 17
Spitfires 13
stations, radar 12, 14-15
Stockport Air Raid Shelters 17

tanks 11, 22, 26

U-boats 9, 24, 25, 30

V1/V2 (flying bombs) 28, 29

Western Approaches 9
Women's Auxiliary Air Force (WAAF) 14, 22, 30
Women's Royal Naval Service (WRNS) 22, 30
work, women's 22-23

X-Craft 25